I0479494

Principles of Building Wealth:

How to Acquire Wealth and Save Money in Tested Ways

By

Robert J. Jones

TABLE OF CONTENTS

Introduction

Investing is the act of allocating resources, such as money or time, with the expectation of generating a profitable return. It involves using cash to purchase assets expected to appreciate over time, generate income, or both. Investors can put their money into a wide range of investment vehicles, such as stocks, bonds, mutual funds, real estate, and alternative investments like commodities and cryptocurrencies. It is also essential to personal finance, allowing individuals to grow their wealth and achieve their financial goals. Whether it's saving for retirement, buying a home, funding education, or building a nest egg, investing is a powerful tool to help people achieve their financial objectives.

It's essential to understand the basics of investing, including the various types of investments, the different investment strategies, and the fundamental principles of risk management. With the proper knowledge and approach, investors can make informed decisions that align with their goals and achieve long-term financial success.

Investing can be a complex and multifaceted field, with numerous strategies and approaches that investors can use to achieve their goals. Some of the most common investment strategies include value investing, growth investing, income investing, and index investing. Each of these strategies involves different approaches to selecting and managing investments and can vary in terms of risk and reward.

Value investing, for example, involves identifying undervalued securities and purchasing them at a discount to their intrinsic value. This strategy can require a significant amount of research and analysis to identify opportunities and may involve investing in companies that are out of favor with the market.

Income investing, as the name suggests, involves investing in assets that generate income, such as dividend paying stocks or bonds. This strategy can be attractive for investors seeking regular income from their investments and may be less volatile than other strategies. Index investing, meanwhile, involves investing in a diversified portfolio of assets that track a specific index, such as the S&P 500. This strategy can provide broad exposure to the market and may be a good option for investors seeking a low-cost, passive approach to investing

Investing involves a range of different asset classes, each with its characteristics and risks. Some of the most common asset classes include stocks, bonds, real estate, commodities, and alternative investments.

Stocks, or equities, are an asset that represents ownership in a company and can provide investors with the potential for long-term growth and capital appreciation. However, they can also be volatile and subject to market fluctuations, making them a higher-risk investment.

Bonds, on the other hand, are debt securities that represent a loan to a company or government entity. They provide investors with regular interest payments and a return of principal at maturity but typically have lower returns than stocks and are subject to interest rate and credit risk.

Real estate can provide investors with the potential for long-term growth and income through rental properties or property appreciation. However, it can also be illiquid and subject to market fluctuations and economic cycles.

Alternative investments include assets like hedge funds, private equity, and cryptocurrencies. These are investments that are often less liquid and more complex than traditional asset classes but can provide diversification and potentially higher returns for investors willing to take on more risk.

When investing, it's essential to consider the specific asset class and underlying investments within that class. For example, when investing in stocks, investors may choose to invest in individual companies or purchase a diversified portfolio of stocks through a mutual fund or exchange-traded fund (ETF)

Chapter 1

Saving

Individuals have diverse definitions of saving. Some people interpret it as saving money in the bank. Others see it as investing in equities or making pension plan contributions. However, saving means one thing to economists: using less of a finite amount of resources now to use more later. Saving is the decision to postpone consumption and store the resulting delayed consumption as an asset.

Saving and investing need clarification, but they are different. Although most consumers consider buying stocks and bonds to be investing, economists define investing as adding to the actual stock of capital, which includes buildings, factories, equipment, and other tangible assets.

Between 1990 and 2005, the annual net national saving rate in the United States (defined as net national income divided by net national income less private consumption expenditures divided by government consumption (Expenditures) was just 5.3 percent. Conversely, the country's savings rate was 7.6% in the 1980s, 10.3% in the 1970s, and 13.0% in the 1960s.

By international and American standards, the U.S. savings rate for 2004 was a startlingly low 2.2%. Comparisons between nations are challenging due to variations in how statisticians define income and consumption in various countries. However, even when these data issues are considered, America's savings rate is much lower than that of other industrialized nations. These largely explain why the United States has recently had a significant current account deficit.

The current account deficit represents a foreign Investment in the United States and less American investment overseas. Americans only save a little; thus, they only have a little money to invest domestically or internationally. Foreigners make up the shortfall by making significant investments in the United States

Inspiration for Saving

People dissave—spend their assets—during retirement from the assets they have accrued via saving and accumulation for their future. A country's saving rate will increase in proportion to the ratio of young savers to aged dissavers. For many years, most economists held that this life-cycle model explained why Americans save. Savings are the primary source of wealth creation in the United

States, which will be left to future generations through bequests or gifts.

Uncertainty surrounds the reasons for elder Americans' bequests and contributions to younger Americans. Since many people only spend their entire savings before passing away, a sizable portion of endowments may be unintentional. In this instance, people save for their consumption rather than to leave a legacy, but they nonetheless end up leaving one.

The retirement funds of elderly Americans in the United States have recently undergone annuity in substantially more significant amounts. In other words, the funds are used to pay regular checks from the employer's social security up to the employee's death, at which point there are no more payments. It is impossible to run the risk of outliving your retirement funds if you receive them as an annuity. People, especially those who have already retired, may have less incentive to save additional money if they "live too long" due to the growing annuity of retirement assets.

One of the main motivations behind saving is the precautionary motive, or the desire to put money away now to be ready for any risks in the future. Along with the danger of outliving their expectations, people save for less exciting hazards like losing their job or paying a lot of uninsured medical expenditures. Studies using computer simulations reveal that the level of precautionary saving might be highly dependent on the availability of insurance against these and other types of risks. An increase of 10% in national savings can be achieved, for instance, by choosing not to insure low-risk but high-cost medical expenses like nursing home care.

The role of the wealthy in producing collective savings is another problem connected to reasons and preferences for saving. Are most Americans who save money wealthy? Actually, no. Some wealthy people save a lot compared to their incomes, whereas others do not. The same is true for the underprivileged. In the United States, wealth can move about a lot, at least over extended periods. The fact that the ranks of the wealthy are constantly shifting shows that while some people who start wealthy lose their fortune, others who start poor save a sizable amount and become wealthy. For instance, during his boxing career, the former heavyweight champion Michael Tyson raked in an estimated $400 million in earnings yet ultimately filed for bankruptcy. Beginning his life in poverty, Sam Walton, the man who founded Wal-Mart, became one of the wealthiest men and women in history.

Economic expansion and population shifts

Savings rates and economic growth are related in a nation. The life-cycle model predicts this. Because of population growth, there will be more young people than older adults, which means that more workers will be saving for retirement than pensioners, who will be dissaving or using up their assets. Overall net savings will be favorable as a result. A higher population growth rate will result in a higher saving rate.

The same is valid for technological advancement. Imagine there are an equal number of young and old individuals worldwide, but due to technological advancement, the young earn more than the old. Then, the young will save more than the elderly, implying a positive savings rate. Over the long term, one should anticipate that there would be no savings in a population or technologically stagnant economy except the savings required to replace depreciating capital. In the long run, if there is no engine for growth, the savings made by the young for retirement, bequests, or any other reason would perfectly balance the savings made by retirees, putting the economy's total savings at zero. Although the level of the economy's positive assets would not change over time, neither would their magnitude.

The absence of long-term savings in an economy does not imply that no one makes long-term savings or spends any savings. It means that the positive savings of those assets that are building up exactly balance the negative savings of those depleting assets. Long-term saving is likely beneficial for growing economies.

Both the number of employees and productivity per employee has significantly increased in recent years. Baby boomers entering the workforce are to blame for the rising number of workers. A growing capital stock, technological advancements, particularly in the information and communications technology sector, and the fact that baby boomers are in their prime years of productivity all contribute to the rise in productivity. The fact that these variables were insufficient to increase U.S. saving rates indicates that other pressures, which will be in more detail below, decreased national savings.

Employment-Related Decisions

The gap between national income and national consumption is the national saving. Approximately 75 percent of the nation's income comes from labor.

Therefore, changes in labor income, if not accompanied by corresponding adjustments in spending, can significantly impact the saving rate of an economy. Consider the striking rise in female labor force participation in the United States over the past few years. In 1975, women between the ages of 25 and 44 made up half of the labor force 1975; by 1988, more than two-thirds were employed. A significant factor, if not the primary factor, in the rise in U.S. per capita income since 1975 is the increase in the female labor supply.

If the asset-increased net-of-tax income these women made had been saved, the U.S. saving rate after 1980 would have exceeded 20%. Since married women, in particular, made up a large amount of the rise in the labor force among women between the ages of eighteen and thirty-five, they would have saved some money for their later years. If this was the case, we need to seek elsewhere to solve the mystery of why saving in the United States decreased.

The increasing rise in the anticipated length of retirement complicates matters. Many Americans, mostly men, are retiring in their late 50s and early 60s. Life expectancy is also increasing concurrently. The average male thirty-year-old now may anticipate living to the age of seventy-six, which is 5.3 years longer than the average thirty-year-old could in 1960. A thirty-year-old today will spend over half his remaining life in retirement if he quits at age fifty-five. According to economic saving models, the total amount saved should be considerably and favorably influenced by the duration of retirement. Therefore, economists anticipate people to save much more money, not much less, as the retirement age is lowering and the average lifespan is rising.

Financial strategy

Government policies can significantly impact the level of savings in a country. To start with, governments themselves are substantial consumers of goods and services. In the U.S., the federal, state, and municipal governments account for more than one-fifth of total consumption. Though it is only sometimes the case that more government consumption spending equals less national saving. The amount of overall savings is unaffected if the private sector cuts back on spending by one dollar in response to a one-dollar increase in government consumption.

The response of the private sector in terms of consumption is highly dependent on who is responsible for funding government spending and how this funding is obtained. Current generations won't have many incentives to cut back on their consumption expenditures, except concern for their offspring, if the government transfers the majority of the tax burden to future generations by borrowing now and repaying principal plus interest on the borrowing in the future.

If current generations are required to foot the bill for government spending, the extent of the private sector's consumption reaction will differ depending on which generation pays the tab. Consumption will decline more significantly the older the taxpaying population becomes. Older adults spend a more considerable proportion of their remaining lifetime resources than younger people since they are closer to the conclusion of their lives. Taxing retirees, for example, rather than employees in their 40s, will thus cause a decline in private-sector consumption and a rise in national savings.

Finally, different taxes have varied effects on incentives. As an illustration, the government might raise money by levying capital gains taxes rather than taxing labor income. Taxes on capital income hinder saving for future consumption, which lowers saving by discouraging it.

Chapter 2

How Much Should You Save?

Do I have enough money saved? Should I be putting away more money? There will be a point when you ask yourself these two questions unless you are an extreme saver. You'll do so for a definite cause if you're like most people.

The National Institute of Statistics estimates that 4.8% of Spanish households save money. Although that percentage is a decent starting point, you might need help to reach your financial objectives, including maintaining a comfortable retirement and creating an emergency fund. What amount should you try to save in the situation? There is no universally applicable fixed proportion.

How Much Should You Save Depending on Your Age and Income?

Throughout a person's life, their income and financial responsibilities change. Both typically get bigger over time. Young people typically have fewer fixed expenses and financial commitments, which allows them more room to save. Unfortunately, your salary can be similarly constrained.

Even though you'll make more money with more experience, it's simple to incur more costs like a mortgage, rent, or children. Does this imply that your rate of savings at 40 will be the same as it was at 20? Nothing can be false.

On the one hand, the amount you save will rise if you continue to save the same percentage of your pay. However, it is revealed that as you age, you will be able to save a more significant proportion of your income.

In addition, everyone should save a minimum amount of money at each stage of their lives per a sound saving strategy.

Savings based on age Minimum 25-year savings period advised: 10%

S25-30 17%

31-35 17%

36-40 15%

41-45 15%

46-50 15%

51-65 15%

Savings based on monthly salary

Net income

Four hundred euros is the minimum amount of savings advised.

10%

401-800

10%

801-1200

15%

1201-1600 15%

1601-2000 17%

2001-3000

17%

3001-4000

17%

>4000 euros 17%

Why Is Saving Money Necessary?

You should develop a good habit of saving early to protect your financial security.

New obstacles are constantly presented in life. You can always be ready for things, even though you cannot forecast them. One of the best things you can do to prepare yourself for life's various challenges is to learn how to save money for unforeseen expenses. Savings can offer you a sense of security and strength that can help you get through difficulties and emergencies and live life to the fullest, but that's not the primary objective. The ultimate objective is for you to be able to use your savings to assist you in reaching milestones or to use when an unexpected event arises, and you urgently need money. If, for instance, you and your spouse are finally prepared to settle down and begin a family, it might feel fantastic to know you're a good steward of your resources. You decide to start looking for a home because your tiny condo only has room for two people and your current pets.

You'll need savings to achieve that, as you might have predicted. You will want funds for closing charges, a down payment, and moving costs. Additionally, to establish a family, you'll need cash for any potential medical expenses and all the equipment you'll need after the kid is born.

How much should I save each month?

Saving money is necessary to achieve financial security for you and your family, but it can be complicated. Your income could stretch between your spending, credit card debt, and other financial commitments.

Whatever the case, you definitely shouldn't put off saving because your life goals might be out of reach without it. To help you with the question, "How much should I save each month?" let's look at the specific reasons you'll want to save money.

It depends on your personal goals, so determine how much of your income you should put aside. Consider your financial objectives' timelines, and then proceed from there.

Both short-term and long-term aims are one example. Less than a year to a few years in the future are considered short-term savings goals. For instance, you may save for a Cancun vacation, a new stove, or a down payment on a home. Retirement and other long-term objectives are things you plan to accomplish after five years.

For these financial objectives, you should consider the precise cash amount and work backward to determine how much you can afford to set down each month. In the following five years, let's suppose you want to have $20,000 for a down payment, $5,000 for a trip to Cancun, and $1,000 for a new stove. It will take $100 per week, or $5,200, to save.

The importance of saving money for an emergency fund is another factor.

Most experts advise increasing your emergency fund until you can cover three to nine months' costs. Please feel free to finish it all simultaneously because it sounds complicated. Even $25 every week is sufficient. Check your budget to see what you can cut (like your cable T.V. bundle), or start packing your lunch more frequently. These two choices, along with others, can have a significant impact.

Savings Programs

It can be helpful to figure out emergency fund and savings targets using the earlier criteria. Here are two rules frequently recommended by financial professionals to aid your savings if you need more guidance (especially if you still need to figure out how much you should set aside each pay period).

The 50/30/20 Principle

The 50/30/20 guideline recommends allocating 50% of your income for necessities like housing, food, and transportation, 30% for discretionary expenses, and 20% for savings.

Use this rule to determine how much you should be saving based on your income. Once you've done that, check to see if your goals align. Consider making it match if it doesn't. If the amount you want to save exceeds 20%? Good news, indeed!

The 10% Rule

Typically, this regulation pertains to retirement savings. According to conventional thinking, you should save 10% of your income for retirement. At first, this number could seem alarming but remember who your employer is when evaluating it. That's because your employer might provide a 401(k) and will match some of your contributions (i.e., free money). Increase your savings rate to 10% as a result. If not, strive to increase your savings until you gradually achieve that amount.

How to Make Savings Grow

It doesn't have to be complicated or painful to increase your savings. Here are some ideas to help you get started: Use automation to your advantage. By routinely sending money from your checking account to a savings account or an IRA, you can start small with an automatic savings plan. Consider requesting that your employer transfer a portion of your earnings into your savings account and the remainder into your checking account. Utilize your tax refunds and bonuses. If you're fortunate enough to receive bonuses at work, think about contributing them to your savings. Alternatively, if you ever receive a tax refund, you can also put that money toward your savings.

By 1% increments, increase your savings. You probably won't notice a significant change in your spending patterns if you allocate an additional 1% of your salary to savings. Increase your savings by 1% when you become accustomed to living without that money, and so on. Beginning a side business Consider a side business to make a little more money if your monthly paycheck is insufficient.

Chapter 3

Where Can I Save Money?

Making a savings decision is difficult. There are several possibilities, all varying in risk. Make sure your money is secure and earn a reasonable interest rate before saving. Some investments gain value relatively quickly, but they can also swiftly lose a significant portion of their value. These investments are referred to as "high risk." It is better to use them once your savings efforts are well underway.

It's wise to keep in mind the adage, "If it sounds too good to be true, it probably is." Promises of swiftly tripling their money have led to the theft of savings from many people. While it is simple to be seduced by promises of financial security, those who participate in "get rich quick" scams typically lose their money very quickly. When you first start saving, invest your funds in secure options like those provided by banks or the post office. Once saving has become a habit, consider alternative investing options. Consider the questions that follow after reading about some of these choices.

1. The piggy bank or mattress method

It is a hazardous approach to saving money. You risk having your money stolen or destroyed if you store it in a piggy bank, under the bed, or in a cabinet. The most significant risk is that you will be tempted to utilize your money, which prevents it from growing because it won't accrue any interest.

2. The savings club approach

A common way to save money is through savings clubs, funeral societies, etc. Most members are close friends, and each makes a monthly contribution. So that saving is made simpler, members support one another. Getting a lump sum out is typically done by members in turn. The savings account often operates on a trust basis and frequently receives no interest. Typically, there are no formal agreements or safeguards to protect your funds from theft. Although you should also have your own savings strategy and accounts, this could be a helpful way to save money for something that will happen soon. For immediate savings, this approach is helpful.

3. A savings account with a bank or post office.

In this way, a person can begin a savings strategy. You can access your savings account with an ATM card, which is relatively simple. You'll need to keep at least some money in it to keep it open. Typically, there are no limitations on when you can withdraw your money. There needs to be more interest earned on savings accounts. This an excellent method to start saving money!

4. Notice payments

A notice deposit will allow you to invest your money at a higher interest rate at the bank or post office. You may need to give the bank the required amount of notice, often 32 or 60 days, depending on the terms of the account, if you want to withdraw your money. Useful for putting money aside in a lump sum you might need later.

5. Fixed Deposit

You could invest a lump sum with your bank or the post office at a greater interest rate if you have saved a particular amount of savings.

As a result, your savings will increase more than they would in a savings account, but you won't be able to access them for a set amount of time, such as six months or a year, depending on the terms—a risk-free strategy for long-term savings.

6. Public Debt

For medium-term savings, bonds are a risk-free, safe option. They are fixed-term investments with a fixed interest rate set when you buy the bond. To avoid paying the penalty, attempt to avoid taking your money out before the maturity date. A wise midterm investment.

7. Pension annuities

There are primarily two methods for saving for retirement. You'll likely be required to join any pension or provident fund your company offers. If not, getting an insurance company's retirement annuity policy is a wise move.

With this contract, you make a monthly payment to the R.A., and the insurance company makes sensible investments to increase it. You will receive a monthly pension for the rest of your life when you retire, typically at age 55 or 60. (At retirement, you will also be able to withdraw 1/3 of your funds in a lump sum.)

Since you can only access this form of savings once you are 55 or 60, it is a great strategy to accumulate funds for your golden years. Before you sign an R.A., make sure you comprehend all of its terms.

8. Unit trusts

You need to gain experience with the stock market to purchase shares and bonds through unit trusts. When you buy and sell bonds and shares, your money is combined with other individuals' money. Unit trusts' value should rise over time when further dividends, interest, and profit are added.

If the shares it has acquired perform poorly or the stock market "crash," unit trust growth is not guaranteed and could fall in value.

You can adjust your savings amount anytime because of a unit trust's high flexibility. Unit trusts may also be sold at any time, although the amount used to buy the stocks and the amount it will sell must be considered. It would help if you spoke with an advisor to determine which unit trust will fit you the most out of the numerous available. If you can afford to take some risks, this is a fantastic strategy to increase your savings.

9. Endowment guidelines

Purchasing an endowment policy from an insurance provider is one approach to setting money aside for a particular objective, such as a car, schooling, or a down payment on a home. The duration of the policy will be fixed, i.e., 5, 10, or more years.

For the policy's term, you pay a certain amount each month, and after that, you will receive a lump sum payment. You must pay a commission to the broker who sold you the insurance coverage because this is a legally enforceable agreement. You will be subject to severe fines if you cancel the coverage before it expires. Although it is not guaranteed, your savings will likely increase in value more than they would in a typical savings or interest-bearing account. Although this investment has more risk, it is a much more disciplined approach to saving money if you are willing to stick with it for the entire time. This is a significant investment, so beware! You will lose if you stop and restart.

10 Justifications for saving money

Why would somebody choose to save money and make a cash purchase when credit is so simple to obtain? If you desire something, you take out your credit card and make payments over an arbitrary period. Everyone pays their bills on time if they can; what's the big deal? Unfortunately, too many individuals understand this way of thinking these days.

1. Achieve Financial Independence

Depending on who you ask, various people have varied standards for what constitutes wealth. But for most people, "being rich" or "wealthy" means having sufficient money and income to live off. Financially speaking, having the flexibility to make decisions unrelated to obtaining a paycheck indicates that you are in charge of your destiny.

This could entail taking vacations whenever you want, quitting your job and returning to school to pursue a different career, starting your own business or investing in someone else's startup, lending a helping hand to family members, accepting a lower-paying position that is more personally fulfilling than financially rewarding, or a popular choice these days: retiring when you want to instead of working because you have to.

Although achieving financial independence does not equate to being wealthy, the freedom from being dependent on a regular paycheck can make you feel incredibly wealthy. Regardless of how you define "wealthy," dependable funds are required.

2. Save 50% on all purchases plus 24% on groceries

If you regularly charge your purchases to your credit card and don't pay it off in full each month, you are likely paying at least 50% extra for everything you buy due to additional interest fees. Break your pricey credit habit by saving money in advance for your expenditures if you depend on your credit cards to support your way of life. Savings allow you to take the time to choose wiser purchases and buy items while they are on sale. People with funds can also purchase large quantities of food while it is on sale (items that are not perishable or which can be frozen). According to one expert, those who practice this may be able to forgo one grocery store visit each month and cut their annual grocery spending by 24%.

3. Purchase a Home

You cannot borrow a down payment; thus, the bank will only loan you money to buy a property if you have one. To avoid being lent money, you must save it or have someone give it to you. Before the bank considers loaning you the remaining 95%, you must put down at least 5% of the home's buying price. You will require an extra 5% merely to cover the various other expenditures and fees associated with purchasing a home, so budget for them. The path to homeownership is paved with savings.

4. Purchase a Car

To obtain a car loan with a fair interest rate, you will need to make a down payment when you want or need to purchase a new vehicle. Of course, you could "borrow" the money from your credit card, but at 20+%, how will that help you succeed? A car loan will undoubtedly cost you something, and it can be a lot, as zero percent financing is only available to stellar customers. The best action is to put aside as much down payment as possible, then weigh your options. Maybe all it takes to get the car you desire is to purchase a good used car rather than a brand-new one.

5. Eliminate Debt

You must have some money saved if you ever want to get out of Debt. It has an ironic ring to it. However, if you keep using credit cards for every "emergency" that arises, they will never be paid off. Statistics suggest that even if you are an excellent planner, half of us incur at least one unforeseen expense each year (half of those will be unexpected car trouble).

Therefore, you should set aside $500 to $1,000 as a reserve fund before you start paying off your credit cards quickly. Then, you can make payments from your reserve fund rather than using your credit cards to pay for unforeseen expenses. You'll be able to tell if your spending is out of control by maintaining a "reserve fund."

6. Annual Costs

To live a good, largely stress-free financial life, you must put money aside each year for your annual costs. These could include funds for gifts, vacations, car upkeep, minor home repairs, appliance repair, property taxes, and income taxes. Refinancing a mortgage or using a line of credit to pay off high-rate credit cards can be engaging ways to pay off Debt, but it is risky to continue putting costs on credit without ever making the payments. Putting money aside in advance is the best method to handle these costs. You'll have peace of mind by doing this and saving money.

7. Unexpected Costs

What would you do if your vehicle required significant repairs? Do you have a stash of $500 to $3,000? What if it is discovered that you are residing in a leaky building or that your home needs some repairs? Bank loans for all of these purposes are only sometimes guaranteed. It is far preferable to prepare for the worst-case scenario and has some money set aside.

8. Emergencies

Even if we all wish they wouldn't, emergencies do occur. You might have to travel urgently, a family member might become ill, and your car might break down or flood your basement, bad weather might cause your pipes to burst, or you might have to fly to a loved one's funeral. We all know that we will have some emergencies from time to time, and any of these situations can be costly. Why not be prepared to avoid becoming a new victim of an emergency?

9. You might lose your job or suffer harm.

When circumstances are good, everyone believes their job is secure, but when things are terrible, many people realize that anything may happen. You could abruptly lose your job, your business could fail, you could suffer a physical or psychological injury, or you could become ill and be unable to work. You are susceptible to any of these events. You must be jobless for six weeks before receiving Employment Insurance (E.I.). Will you rely on borrowing to make ends meet, or do you have enough savings to last? Living on credit may easily make a poor situation even worse in a time like this. Minimum payments rise until they become unmanageable and credit limits stop adjusting. Then, when you do finally start making money, what used to be enough to get by doesn't anymore since you have so many new debt payments to make every month. Since you will need to pay off your obligations someday, you require more money than you did previously.

10. Live a Happy Life

Living constantly under stress and hand-to-mouth has profound emotional, psychological, and bodily repercussions. People who don't make plans appear to jump from crisis to catastrophe.

Uncommon knowledge holds that being organized can make you happier. Being organized can assist, but it will make you miserable. Setting away money to use when necessary is essentially arranging and taking charge of your future and financial matters because so many aspects of your future are outside your control. With savings, you have nothing to lose and only a happier future to gain.

Specific Steps for Saving

Setting goals is the next step to staying on track after realizing the value of saving and its part in your life. Making sure you can achieve your financial goals is necessary for goal-setting. You could utilize an online savings calculator to ensure your demands match your plan.

Now that you have the knowledge and resources to set practical financial goals, it's time to identify and commit the funds necessary to achieve your objectives.

1. Create a budget

You should first create and adhere to a budget. This entails being honest and realistic about your household's financial condition as well as creating spending goals that are reasonable and attainable so that you can save. It needs to be more to promise to save and to consider saving merely. You'll need to make wise financial decisions.

2. Comprehend the idea of cash flow

It will help if you understand cash flow, including what it is, how it operates, and how much money you spend on living expenses. Look over your income and expenses to determine your spending patterns. Make changes to what you can with intention so that you have money accessible for saving.

3. Cooperate with your companion

Collaboration and communication are essential when managing your home finances if you're married or living with someone else. Your ambitions, plans, and financial resources must all be shared to save. Even the best-laid plans will only be successful if everyone is involved.

4. Differentiate "Want" from "Need."

Recognize the distinctions between necessities and wants, then list your own. You can decline offers when they conflict with your present and long-term financial objectives.

5. Implement automation

Save money by automating saves. If you wait until the month's end to save, much won't be left. Set it up so that money is automatically deducted from your paycheck and deposited, or set it up so that a portion goes into a savings account whenever you make a deposit. If you have several savings goals, you can keep note of the money you deposit into one account and transfer it to another, or you can keep several different savings accounts open for varied purposes. You are more inclined to maintain your savings when seeing them increase.

6. Do an evaluation.

We may only be aware of what they are once we consider our monthly expenses. Review all of the purchases you make. What is not necessary that you are purchasing? Is it cheaper if you do need it?

7. Find areas where you can cut

How can you improve your savings goals by reducing what costs or purchases you make? Energy and utility costs, food and grocery costs, bank and credit card fees, taxes, and auto expenses are the five main areas to look at for opportunities.

8. Consider the kids

Remember to consider your kids, too. It is crucial to instill in children the values of saving and spending. Furthermore, you must lead by example since people will imitate your actions and follow your lead on how important money is in your life. Some essential skills are waiting to buy something you want, creating particular strategies for kids to save, making good decisions, and realizing that it cannot be spent again.

9. Begin now

Always start now, no matter what your objective may be. There will always be something vying for your resources. Whatever comes up, you should always keep saving for the future at the top of your financial and mental priorities.

10. Relish life.

Yes, we have been extolling the benefits of self-control, cutting back, and delaying gratification. But we're all just people. While it's essential to save money, it's also okay to occasionally treat yourself to something fun, relaxing, for a celebration, or just for the fun of it. The occasional indulgence should, however, be planned for in your budget.

Chapter 4

Five Strategies for Guilt-Free Spending

We've all been there—guilt every time we swipe another card at a store. Putting a last-minute, inexpensive flight ticket on your credit card and simultaneously being hit with a sense of exhilaration and remorse.

Let's be clear: having some guilt after spending money isn't always a terrible thing. Doing so might mean surrendering our goals, going over our budget, or simply spending money we don't have.

Controlling our guilt over spending and money is critical to mending our connection with them. We shouldn't dodge money.

You shouldn't feel bad about spending your money, whether you immediately regretted it or loved it but felt bad about how much it cost you.

1. Establish a budget that is suitable for you

Budgeting is the first item on our list because it forms the basis of your financial planning. Budgets are not meant to impose limitations. Instead, they are meant to assist you in understanding and assessing your relationship with money. Instead of making you feel too constrained, they need to aid you in achieving your objectives.

The zero-based budget, which gives each dollar a "task," is comparable to how most people conceptualize a budget. If that seems too demanding, consider a budget that pays you first or follows the 50/30/20 or envelope systems. Budgets are adaptable. Your budget from the previous year could not be effective for you in the coming one. For a month, your categories appeared one way, but your current priorities have changed. You may have had more time to devote to budgeting the previous year, but you want something more automatic this year.

A budget requires trial and error to find what works best for you. Once you've found a budget that works for you, you must have faith that you've made it to satisfy your requirements, aspirations, and objectives.

2. Prioritize your values

Prioritizing your values will make your budget less constricting and more aligned with your goals and way of life. Additionally, it can ensure that you engage in guilt-free spending.

Spending that is motivated by values is when you do so. You can use the following inquiries to determine your values for this kind of planning:

• What brings you joy?
• What would you like to do more of?
• When do you become the giddiest?
• What kind of change would you like to contribute?
What saps your strength or joy?
You'll see that the secret is to figure out what experiences—or potential expenditures—make your life happier. This is distinct from impulsive spending, which may feel wonderful at the time but lacks the thought and consideration that value-based spending encourages.

3. Establish Sinking Funds

Sinking funds are an effective technique to put value-based spending principles into practice. They differ from common savings goals in that you contribute a specific amount on a predetermined timetable based on how long it will take you to attain your goal.

Let's say you enjoy traveling and are sick of feeling bad when you make hasty airfare purchases that you can't truly afford. Consider prioritizing travel by putting certain value-based financial habits into place. The next time you see a cheap hotel or ticket listing, you can take advantage of it guilt-free because you have occasionally set money aside for this occasion.

4. Spending money for "fun."

It's important to think about and plan for our first three suggestions. In truth, we are aware that our spending habits, needs, and desires are not always predictable. However, even in this case, we can take measures to prevent our wallets from being destroyed by this "uncontrolled" spending.

After meeting your savings objectives and covering your essential costs, you'll know how much "fun money" you have. Fun money is money that will be spent in a variety of ways. Although you know you cannot plan for everything, fun money is scheduled.

You won't feel bad ordering food from your favorite restaurant the next time you're fatigued after a difficult day because you can do it with part of your "fun money."

5. Hold on a moment.

This may assist with the immediate need to pause, but it may also help you become more conscious of which of your impulses are strongest and most frequently manifest. While making a list is one method to practice greater pause and contemplation in your spending, it is only one way. Other options include:

- Making a circuit of the store.
- Keeping the item with you until you're ready to stand in line.
- Enforcing a 24-hour rule for purchases over a specific threshold.

There are countless options available to you. Doing this can reduce the immediate guilt that could come after making a large "YOLO" purchase and help develop more guilt-free purchasing habits.

Chapter 5

Should You Ever Get in Debt?

No debt, after all, is a good debt, according to some. However, many people can only afford to buy big-ticket items like a home by borrowing money and taking on debt. Most of the time, those types of loans are acceptable and provide value to the borrower, but there is also the opposite end of the spectrum where reckless borrowing is concerned. Between these two extremes, it's simple to draw a distinction; other debts, however, are more challenging to evaluate.

Key Takeaway

• Good debt has the potential to boost your net worth or significantly improve your life.

• Bad debt refers to borrowing money solely for consumption or to buy quickly depreciating assets.

• Depending on an individual's financial status, including how much they can afford to lose, it might be difficult to tell whether a debt is good or bad.

What is good debt?

It is said that "it takes money to make money" is a common example of good debt. Debt that significantly enhances your life and the lives of your family members might also do this. These are some of the things that are frequently worthwhile to incur debt for:

• Education. Generally speaking, a person's earning potential increases with education level. The likelihood of finding employment is positively correlated with education. Workers with more education are more likely to have well-paying jobs and often have an easier time finding new ones if the need arises. A college or technical degree investment can frequently pay for itself within a few years of beginning a job. For any topic of study that appeals to you, it is important to consider both the short- and long-term possibilities because not all degrees are created equal.

• You run your own business. Good debt can also include money you borrow to launch your own business. Being your employer can frequently be financially and psychologically gratifying. It may also need a lot of laborious work. Starting your own business carries risks, much like paying for school. Although many businesses fail, your chances of success are higher if you choose a subject that you are knowledgeable about and passionate about.

• Your residence or other real property. Real estate offers many opportunities for financial gain. In terms of housing, the simplest frequently is obtaining a mortgage to purchase a home, residing there for a while, and then selling the home for a profit. Along with the freedom of owning your own home, you may also be eligible for some tax benefits that are not accessible to renters. If you know what you're doing, renting out residential real estate can also be a source of income, cash flow, and potential capital gains.

What Is a Bad Debt?

It is typically considered bad debt if you borrow money to buy a declining asset. Put another way, and you should only incur debt to purchase something if it increases in value or produces revenue. Examples include

• Cars. Even if you might find it impossible to live without a car, it isn't wise to borrow money to get one. The car already has a lower value when you leave the dealership than when you first acquired it. If you need a loan to purchase a car, seek one with a low or no interest rate. Even though you won't pay interest, you will still be investing a sizable sum in a declining asset.

• Consumables and apparel. It's commonly believed that clothing costs only about 50% of what people pay. The phrase "half" is being generous, as you can observe by glancing around a used clothing store. Unwise use of debt would be to use a high-interest credit card to borrow money to pay for necessities like clothing, food, and furnishings. Utilize a credit card for convenience, but be sure you can pay off the entire sum at the end of the month to avoid interest costs. Otherwise, try paying with cash.

Cardholders are given an additional incentive to spend through credit card reward schemes. However, keep in mind that if you don't pay off your debt in full each month, the interest fees may outweigh the value of your incentives.

Unique Considerations

Debt is only sometimes as readily categorized as beneficial or negative. It frequently is based on your financial condition or other variables. Some forms of debt may be beneficial to some people while being detrimental to others:

• Borrowing money to settle a debt. Customers currently in debt may find it advantageous to obtain a debt consolidation loan from a bank or another trustworthy lender. Since debt consolidation loans often have lower interest rates than most credit cards, you can use them to pay off current bills and reduce future interest costs. Make sure you use the money to pay off debts rather than other expenses. Investopedia presents ratings of the top debt consolidation loans that are frequently updated.

• Borrowing to make investments. If you have a brokerage account, you can access a margin account, which enables you to borrow money from the brokerage to buy stocks. When you purchase securities on margin, you can profit (should the asset increase in value before the loan must be repaid) or lose money (if the security loses value). This type of borrowing is not appropriate for novice investors or those who cannot afford to lose some money.

You may hear that getting into debt is something you should never do since it is risky. Some people think that once you start piling up debt, it will be impossible for you to escape it and that your financial situation will be irreparably damaged.

To remark that you shouldn't use a chainsaw because you could lose an arm is analogous. True, you should only use a chainsaw if you have had training or are responsible around them. However, a chainsaw is a tool, just like any other, and if you know how to use it correctly and when to use it, you can prune your trees while keeping all of your arms and legs intact when you're finished. Similarly, consider your debt. If you're clever and disciplined enough to know how to utilize it correctly, it's another tool in your financial arsenal that can be helpful to you.

"Debt can be utilized wisely, so it helps cover unexpected needs and offers an opportunity to build your credit history with a record of on-time payments and acceptable debt management," said Bruce McClary, vice president of communications for the National Foundation for Credit Counseling. The best method to maintain good credit and keep debt within your means is to make on-time payments and keep balances modest compared to credit limitations. So, how do you manage debt effectively? You should keep in mind three key guidelines.

Rule No. 1: Avoid increasing your expenses through debt
Some people borrow money to purchase luxury goods like jewelry or an automobile they otherwise couldn't afford. That is a bad concept. It would be best if you didn't use

debt to purchase something you don't need to increase your monthly expenses.

One person is exempt from this rule. Increasing your expenses through debt may be okay if you receive a long-term asset in exchange. For instance, if you take out a mortgage to buy a house, the mortgage payment would increase your monthly expenses. However, as you continue to make that payment, the bank's ownership of a permanent asset (your house) decreases, and your share increases.

Keep in mind that I indicated it might be acceptable to do this. You don't want to purchase a home that is so expensive that your monthly mortgage payment will be unaffordable.

According to McClary, debt can become an increasingly severe problem with long-lasting effects "at any point where it becomes unmanageable, and, likely, a payment will not be made on time."

You must be able to repay your loan on time, even if you receive something long-lasting in return. In a moment, we'll discuss that.

However, only some individuals are purchasing homes amid the pandemic. (Well, some of them are, but that's another story for another week.) Many people are in survival mode, only trying to maintain a minimal cash flow until employment arises again. It is anticipated that you will find a new job or, if you manage a small business, your clients will return within a few months or weeks. Until then, you must temporarily take care of your basic needs.

It seems sensible to take on debt once you've reduced your expenses as much as possible to meet any minimum costs that remain, provided that you're just doing it temporarily to get by on the essentials.

Rule No. 2: Reduce the expense of your debt.

You might believe that your monthly payment constitutes the "cost" of your debt. For instance, if your credit card's minimum monthly payment is $125, your debt must cost you $125 each month.

Nope. Monthly payment amounts can be quite deceptive. Simply by extending the time you have to repay your loan, banks can cut your monthly payment. When you're strapped for cash, that could be useful, but the cost will rise over time.

The two most crucial figures for your debt are the interest rate and the fees, which you should find instead of the monthly payment. You should try to keep both of them as low as possible because they will both cost you money. Imagine that you are getting unemployment benefits, have already reduced your spending, and still require an additional $350 per month for the next six months to cover your essential expenses. Because $350 times six is $2,100, you decide to use a credit card to pay for the extra $350 each month. As a result, you rack up $2,100 in debt. You decide its okay to get into debt because it costs $52 a month because that is the minimum payment your bank requires on your $2,100 balance. However, your payment is a mere $52 a month because your bank is forcing you to pay just 1% of the debt each month while also assessing an insane 18% interest rate annually.

Even if you continue making payments of $52 a month, it would still take you more than five years to pay off the full $2,100. Additionally, you will wind up paying more than $1,100 in interest, which is more than 50% of the original loan amount. The total cost of your loan includes that amount and any additional costs your bank may impose along the route.

What would be a better course of action? Get a new credit card with a 0% introductory interest rate on purchases if your credit is good. According to Schulz, zero-percent deals might be a real blessing for people in debt.

Rule No. 3: Plan to pay off the debt before accepting the funds.

Taking on debt without a plan for repaying it is a common error people make. With credit cards, this occurs frequently. People use credit cards to make more purchases than they can afford, then they start making minimum payments rather than paying off the balance promptly. Eventually, they will make payments at a rate at which it will take years to repay the entire balance. How many outcomes can be avoided? Make a repayment strategy for any debt you intend to incur before you take it on.

As a result, if you're using a credit card with 0% interest to finance your debt, you'll need to calculate how much you need to spend each month to pay off the majority or all of it before the intro period expires.

Let's examine a further illustration. Take a peek at your monthly statement and check for a box that resembles this if you have any balance on your credit card.

Every bank is required by law to include a section like this on credit card statements so that customers can see how much their debt costs. I used a 0% balance transfer offer to consolidate $10,000 in debt onto a single credit card; thus, this particular box belongs to me. I have been assessed a 2% fee, so my initial debt balance is $10,200, and I'll have 12 months of 0% interest.

This box now indicates that my bank requires a minimum payment of $102 per month to begin. But have a look at the red-highlighted section. It will take me an absurd 29 years to pay off this $10,000 debt if I make the minimum payment going forward. In addition, because my interest rate will increase once my introductory offer expires in a year, I'll pay about $13,000 in interest throughout the loan.

Crazy, huh? Debt can become unmanageable in this manner. However, making a strategy to pay more than the required minimum payment each month is the answer. The box illustrates what would occur if I paid a greater monthly amount of $337 instead of simply the minimum. If I do that, I'll pay off the entire $10,000 in about three years, and the interest will only total about $2,000. However, there is still a lot of curiosity, so I'll go even further. I'm coming up with a plan to pay off this debt for $500 each month. Since if I do that, I'll finish paying off $6,000 before my 12-month period of 0% interest expires.

Then, I'll try to transfer the remaining debt to a different credit card with a new 0% interest offer and pay off the balance that way.

A strategy that pays off all of your debt during the introduction time is ideal, provided you can do so. I made a compromise at $500 each month because, for this $10,000, that would equal $833 a month, which is quite pricey. Even at that pace, I won't be in as bad of a situation a year from now because I won't owe nearly $9,000 like I would if I only made the minimum payment, but rather only about $4,200.

Yes, discipline is necessary to follow through on a plan. It's easy to imagine that everything will be fine as long as you pay the minimum payment. Even if it is a stretch, you must plan your monthly budget to include the additional sum. The expense of your debt must be known in advance so that you may create a solid plan to minimize it to a minimum.

Finally, pay attention if you're having trouble managing your debt. "Call and request assistance from your credit card issuer if the infection has turned your financial life upside down," suggested Schulz. "Issuers have what are known as hardship programs designed to assist people with temporary challenges that are not their fault."

In addition, get help if the thought of speaking with your bank makes you uneasy. McClary suggested that if dealing with these issues on your own proves to be difficult that you seek free advice from a nonprofit credit counseling organization. "A qualified credit counselor can assist you in developing a realistic budget and identifying strategies for paying down your debt on an affordable basis."

Use debt as a temporary fix, not a crutch.
Normally, it isn't a good idea to use debt to make up the difference if your income is limited. But the economic situation we're facing is unprecedented. It's realistic to believe that if you recently lost your job or had your hours reduced, your financial situation will improve over the next 12 months. While it's not the ideal answer, using debt to bridge the gap can be effective if you do it correctly. Debt can assist you in getting through difficult times if used wisely as a temporary cure. However, it's crucial to only incur debt for necessities rather than indulgences, be aware of your debt's true cost, and have a repayment strategy in place before you begin. If you adhere to these three guidelines, you can use debt to your advantage without risking serious injury.

Chapter 6

How to Save for a Down Payment

According to conventional opinion, the homeowner will benefit more from making a larger down payment since he will have more equity in the home when he moves in. But how does one begin saving for this required down payment? You can use the advice below to make this task simpler:

Use the 50-30-20 strategy.

It would be best if you had the financial discipline to save for the down payment. One strategy is to stick to a 50-30-20 budget, where 50% of your take-home pay should be set aside for fixed needs, 30% for other discretionary expenses and 20% should unquestionably be saved. Cutting out on amenities you may otherwise be able to afford will be complex, but it will be well worth the effort once you move into your new house.

Think about drastically altering your way of life.

You should consider making significant changes to your life if you are truly devoted to saving for and purchasing your own home. One way to do it is to temporarily move into a smaller apartment, which will enable you to save at least 20% of the money you spend on rent. In addition to your normal job, consider other sources of income. Doing both will help you save for that down payment on your home while living within your means and reducing expenses like vacations, entertainment, and subscriptions you could live without for at least two to three years.

Generating income from your other assets

If you want to buy your own home, you should start saving for it three to four years in advance. However, if you haven't already, consider selling some of your other investments to make the down payment. Either withdraw money from a fixed deposit or take out a loan against a life insurance policy. You may be able to borrow up to 85–90% of the surrender value, depending on the rules set forth by your insurance provider. You can pay off this loan in full when it matures or in two equal payments every six months. The interest rate for the same could be in the region of 9–10%. The best ways to raise cash for a down payment on a home are those mentioned above. Due to the astronomical interest rates they would incur, credit cards and personal loans should always be avoided. Over time, this would increase your debt load. In the end, you should be aware that saving for a down payment is a challenging undertaking and that there is no substitute for financial discipline when it comes to doing so.

Chapter 7

When can I start my retirement?

When to retire is a personal decision based on a variety of elements, including your financial situation and risk tolerance. It's crucial to take into account how your retirement age may affect the size of your benefit. When can I retire? Is this a question that must be answered by contrasting anticipated expenses with anticipated income? Young people have to make educated guesses. But when you're only ten years from retiring, you ought to know considerably more about those figures. The questions to which you must respond to determine when you can retire are listed below.

First, money

How much social security will I receive?

In 2021, the average monthly social security benefit was $1,543, while at full retirement age, the maximum social security benefit was $3,148, and when someone turns 70, the maximum benefit is $3,895.

• Social Security retirement payments can be received as early as age 62, but there will be a permanent reduction in your benefits of between 25% and 30% from what you would receive at full retirement age.

The present full retirement age is 66; however, that age will soon increase to 67 for those born after 1960.

• The maximum Social Security benefit is 70 years old. Your paychecks could be up to 76% larger than what you would receive at 62 and between 24% and 32% larger than what you would receive at full retirement age.

. Benefits from Social Security increase by 5% to 8% for every year you wait. That's an exceptional guaranteed return; therefore, many financial advisors advise working longer or using other retirement savings if you can delay applying.

Chapter 8

What Is Investing?

In general, investing means putting money to work overtime in a project or endeavor to generate profits (i.e., profits exceeding the initial investment). It is allocating resources, typically capital (i.e., money), to produce income, profits, or gains.

One can engage in various activities (directly or indirectly), such as utilizing funds to launch a business or buying assets like real estate to earn rental income or resell it at a higher price in the future.

The difference between investing and saving is that when you invest, you put your money to work, which means there is an implicit risk that the related project(s) could fail and cause you to lose money. In contrast to investing, speculation is wagering on short-term price swings rather than putting money to work per se.

The difference between investing and saving is that when you invest, you put your money to work, which means there is an implicit risk that the related project(s) could fail and cause you to lose money. In contrast to investing, speculation is wagering on short-term price swings rather than putting money to work per se.

Knowing about Investing

A person invests to increase their money over time. The fundamental tenet of investing is the expectation of a favorable return in income or price appreciation with statistical significance. There is a fairly broad range of assets in which one can invest and generate a return.

In investment, risk and return are inversely correlated; low risk typically translates into low predicted returns, whereas larger profits are typically associated with increased risk. Basic investments like Certificates of Deposit (CDs) are at the low end of the risk spectrum; bonds or fixed-income instruments are at the higher end, and stocks or equities are considered riskier. Generally speaking, commodities and derivatives are among the riskiest investments. Another option for investing is in something tangible like real estate or land or something fragile like fine art and antiques.

Risk and return expectations differ greatly within the same asset class. Asset types have an impact on the returns they produce. Bonds pay interest every three months, whereas many stocks pay quarterly dividends. Various forms of income are taxed at various rates in many different jurisdictions.

In addition to regular revenue like dividends or interest, price growth is a significant factor in return. Thus, the total return on investment is income plus capital growth. According to Standard & Poor's calculations, since 1926, capital gains have generated two-thirds of the total equity return for the S&P 500, while dividends have contributed about a third. Investments are crucial, and capital gains are one of them.

Investment Categories

Investments are typically considered today as financial tools that enable people or organizations to raise and allocate cash to businesses. These businesses than invest that money and put it to use for expansion or profit-making ventures.

Despite the vastness of the investment world, these are some of the more popular ones.

Stocks

A purchaser of a firm's stock becomes a fractional company owner Shareholders are those who own stock in a company, and they can benefit from that firm's expansion and success by increasing the value of their shares and receiving regular dividends from the company's earnings.

Bonds

Bonds are debt obligations issued by governments, municipalities, and enterprises. A bond means that you own a portion of a company's debt and are qualified to receive periodic interest payments and the face value of the bond when it matures.

Funds

Investing in commodities, preferred shares, stocks, bonds, and other assets is made possible via funds, which are pooled vehicles managed by investment managers. Mutual and exchange-traded funds (ETFs) are the most popular funds. Investors trade on stock exchanges and, like stocks, are valued continuously throughout the trading day, unlike mutual funds, which do not trade on an exchange and are evaluated at the close of the trading day. The S&P 500 or the Dow Jones Industrial Average are indices that mutual funds and different investors can either passively track or actively manage.

Alternative investing strategies

Hedge funds and private equity fall under the umbrella of alternative investments." Hedge funds are so named because they can utilize long and short positions in stocks and other investments to diversify their investing bets. Without becoming public, private equity helps businesses to raise money. Hedge funds and private equity were traditionally only accessible to wealthy investors referred to as "accredited investors" and meet specific income and net worth standards. Alternative investments have, however, recently been made available to retail investors in the form of funds.

Options and Other Derivatives

Financial derivatives derive their value from another instrument, such as a stock or index. Options contracts are a common derivative that provides the buyer the right, but not the duty, to buy or sell a security at a fixed price within a certain time frame. Derivatives frequently use leverage, making them high-risk, high-reward investments.

Commodities

Financial instruments, currencies, metals, oil, grains, and animal products are some the examples of commodities. They can be traded through ETFs or commodity futures, which are contracts to purchase or sell a specific amount of a commodity at a defined price on a specific future date. Both risk hedging and speculative uses of commodities are possible.

Let's contrast a few of the most popular investing approaches:

• **Active vs. passive investing:** Active investing seeks to outperform the market by actively managing the investment portfolio. In contrast, passive investors support a passive strategy, such as purchasing an index fund, in an implicit admission that it is challenging to outperform the market continuously. Both strategies have advantages and disadvantages, but in practice, only a few fund managers routinely outperform their benchmarks, which makes active management more expensive.

• **Value vs. growth:** Value companies often have lower price-earnings (P/E) ratios than high-growth corporations, which growth investors prefer. Firms with PE ratios that are much lower than growth businesses and dividend yields that are higher than those of growth companies are the ones that value investors choose to invest in because they may be temporarily or permanently unpopular with investors

Chapter 9

How to Invest: Do-It-Yourself Investing

The answer to "how to invest" depends on whether you are a do-it-yourself (DIY) investor or would rather have a professional manage your money. Due to the low commissions and simplicity of trading on their platforms, many investors who prefer to manage their own money have accounts at a discount or online brokerages. Self-directed investing, often known as DIY investing, calls for a significant bit of knowledge, aptitude, time commitment, and emotional restraint. It could be wiser to let a professional help handle your finances if these qualities don't accurately represent you.

Professionally Managed Investing

Wealth managers typically look after the investments of investors who desire professional money management. As part of their standard fee structure, wealth managers typically charge their clients a proportion of the assets they are managing. Although hiring a professional money manager costs more than managing money on one's own, many investors are willing to pay for the ease of having an expert handle the research, investment decisions, and trading.

Investors are advised to verify that their investment professional is duly registered and licensed by the SEC's Office of Investor Education and Advocacy.

Robotic Advisory Investing

Some investors choose to make investments based on recommendations from computerized financial advisors. Robotic advisors, powered by computers and artificial intelligence, compile essential data about the investor and their risk profile to make relevant recommendations. Robotic investment advisors (robotic advisors) provide services akin to human investment advisors at a lower cost with little human intervention. Robotic advisors can now do more than just choose investments, thanks to technological improvements. They can aid in the creation of retirement plans, the management of trusts, and the administration of other retirement accounts like 401(k).

An Overview of Investing History

While investing has been around for millennia, the modern form of investing can be traced back to the 17th and 18th centuries when the first public markets were established and connected individuals with investment opportunities. The Amsterdam Stock Exchange and the New York Stock Exchange (NYSE) were founded in 1602.

Aspects of the Industrial Revolution

People accrued funds that might be invested due to the improved wealth brought about by the Industrial Revolutions of 1760–1840 and 1860–1914, which encouraged the growth of a sophisticated banking system. Most well-known banks that rule the financial sector, such as Goldman Sachs and J.P. Morgan, started in the 1800s.

20th Century Investing

With the creation of fresh ideas in asset pricing, portfolio theory, and risk management, the 20th century saw significant advancements in investing theory. Hedge funds, private equity, venture capital, REITs, and ETFs are just a few innovative investment vehicles created in the second half of the 20th century.

The democratization of investment, which had begun more than a century earlier, was completed in the 1990s thanks to the Internet's rapid expansion, which made online trading and research skills available to the general people.

The 21st Century Investing

The dot.com boom, which made a new generation of billionaires from investments in stocks of technology-driven and online businesses, burst at the beginning of the twenty-first century, ushering in the era and possibly laying the groundwork for what was to come. Enron's bankruptcy in 2001, which left the company, its accounting firm, Arthur Andersen, as well as many of its investors broke, thrust the collapse of the company into the spotlight.

The Great Recession (2007-2009), when an enormous number of failed investments in mortgage-backed securities damaged economies worldwide, is one of the most notable events of the twenty-first century, or history for that matter. Well-known banks and investment companies failed, foreclosed homes increased, and the wealth disparity worsened.

Through the proliferation of low-cost online investment firms and free trading apps, the 21st century also made investing accessible to beginners and unconventional investors.

Exactly how do I begin investing?

Utilizing the assistance of a financial expert, such as a broker or advisor. Understanding your preferences and risk tolerance is crucial before investing. The best solution is not to invest in stocks and options if you are risk-averse. Create a plan that details your investment goals and frequency. You have the option of doing it yourself, choosing investments based on your investing style, or hiring a professional investor and having them recommend investments based on your tastes and goals. Research the potential investment carefully to ensure it aligns with your plan and can produce the required results before devoting your money. There is a need for you to know that you don't need a lot of money to start and that you can adapt as your needs change.

How Can Invest Help My Funds Grow?

Investments are not only for the wealthy. You can make little investments. You may, for instance, buy inexpensive stocks, put tiny sums of money into a savings account that pays interest, or save up until you have the desired sum to invest. Set aside small sums from your pay if your employer provides a retirement plan, such as a 401(k), until you can increase your investment. Your investment might have doubled if your employer takes part in matching programs.

Open an IRA or start investing in stocks, bonds, mutual funds, etc. It's nothing to sneeze at to start with $1,000. Millions would be earned now from a $1,000 investment in Amazon's IPO in 1997. Multiple stock splits had a significant role in this, but it makes no difference to the outcome—impressive returns. Most financial organizations provide savings accounts, which can be opened with little initial investment. In general, savings accounts don't offer high-interest rates, so compare your options to choose one with the finest features and most affordable rates.

$1,000 can be used to make a real estate investment. Even if you cannot purchase an income-producing property, you can invest in a business that does. A business that invests in and manages real estate to increase profits and generate income is known as a real estate investment trust (REIT). You can put $1,000 in mutual funds, exchange-traded funds, or REIT stock.

Is investing the same as gambling?

They have nothing to do with one another. As a result, they are very different. When you invest, you put your money to work in ventures or pursuits with positive expected returns or returns that will be positive over the long term. Betting on the results of events or games is known as gambling. Your money isn't even being used. Gambling frequently has a negative expected return. Even though an investor could lose money, it will do so because the enterprise doesn't succeed. The outcome of gambling, on the other hand, is completely dependent on chance.

Stocks, bonds, mutual funds, and real estate are examples of the various investment vehicles available. Each one has a unique set of risks and potential benefits.
Investors have two options: they can invest on their own, without the assistance of a professional, or they can use a registered and qualified investment advisor. Investing solutions that are automated can now be provided to investors via Robo-advisors thanks to technology.
The amount of capital, or money, needed to invest primarily relies on the type of investment and the investor's financial situation, objectives, and aspirations.

Meanwhile, more people can now join as the number of vehicles has dropped below their entry thresholds. Always do your homework before investing, regardless of how or what you decide to invest in. This goes for your target as well as your investment manager or platform. "Never invest in a business you cannot comprehend" is arguably one of the best advice, according to seasoned and successful investor Warren Buffet.

Chapter 10

Why should you invest?

Investing is the best method to make your money work for you and accumulate wealth. Although keeping money in cash or bank savings accounts is a safe strategy, investing enables it to increase in value over time with the advantages of compounding and long-term growth. Investing aims to enhance value and equity, create wealth, and generate future income. You can invest in stocks, bonds, mutual funds, options, futures, precious metals, real estate, or small businesses.

Different factors influence why people invest. Let's examine a few:

1. Financial stability: People need additional cash because they wish to be financially stable. They can safeguard their finances from any financial difficulties that may arise. An expensive life event, such as a serious health issue, the devastation of a home by a typhoon, or a fire, could serve as an illustration. Your financial security to handle such unforeseen catastrophes is ensured by having an investments

2. Financial autonomy: Your investment allows you to be self-sufficient and avoid depending on other people's funds in a financial emergency. It guarantees you will have enough money to support your needs and wants for the rest of your life without needing to rely on others or work as you age.

3. Increase your fortune: People invest in increasing their wealth. In other words, they gradually invest their savings after they save. The investment earnings, including dividends and interest, may be reinvested in the same financial instrument or even something else during this procedure. In this manner, you, too, can begin investing and carry on increasing your fortune.

4. Achieve your objectives: Some people invest to achieve specific life goals that they have set. The objective you choose would be your reason to invest, for instance, if you wanted to buy a house, a new automobile, or go on an international vacation. It's crucial to make a list of your objectives and the amount of money required to reach each. You could have short-term, medium-term, or long-term objectives. Your ability to increase your money and fast reach your goals without working a lifetime will depend on how you invest it following your aims.

Why Investing is Important at Any Age

Age, income, and risk profiles are just a few variables that can affect a person's aspirations. The following three categories further divide age:
• Young and beginning a career
• Family-building in middle age
• Retirement age and self-directed

These segments frequently fall short at the right time, with middle-aged people thinking about investments for the first time or the elderly being forced to budget and develop the discipline they had as young adults.

Since you cannot invest what you do not have, income is the logical starting point for investment planning. A young adult's first job serves as a wake-up call, forcing judgments concerning IRA contributions, savings accounts, or money market accounts, as well as the sacrifices needed to balance growing affluence with the demand for immediate gratification. Refrain from stressing out too much over failures during this time, such as feeling overwhelmed by your automobile and school loan payments or forgetting that your parents no longer pay the monthly credit card bill.

The choices we make that affect wealth management are determined by our outlook, which also establishes the playing field on which we compete throughout our lives. For many people, planning a family comes first. Couples decide how many children they want, where they want to live, and how much money is necessary to achieve those aspirations. These calculations are frequently complicated by career expectations, with individuals with advanced degrees enjoying more earning potential and those stuck in low-paying professions having to make sacrifices to make ends meet.

There is always a good time to start investing. Before you realize that life is going swiftly and that you must make arrangements for retirement and old age, you can be well into middle age. When setting investment goals too late, fear may take over, but fear should vanish once the strategy is in motion. Regardless of your age, income, or mindset, always remember that all investments begin with the first dollar. However, people who invest for a long time have an edge since their wealth grows, enabling them to live a lifestyle that others cannot.

Reasons why you shouldn't choose individual stocks

Years ago, I quit choosing particular stocks, and I suggest you do the same. However, I will present a fresh justification today rather than the conventional one for why you shouldn't choose stocks. The conventional wisdom is that since most people—including experts—cannot beat the index, there is no point in making an effort. You have probably heard this argument before.

I'll make a case for picking individual stocks instead. It usually takes little time to determine whether someone is skilled in a given field.

For instance, any effective basketball coach could tell you within the first 10 minutes whether a player was a skilled shooter. Yes, it is possible to strike it fortunate and make a lot of shots in the beginning, but soon they will go toward their actual shooting percentage. A technical field like computer programming is no different. A skilled coder could identify someone who lacks subject matter expertise within a short period.

However, how about stock picking? How long would it take to establish someone's stock-picking skill?

One hour? A week? A year?

Even after trying for several years, you could not be certain. Compared to other disciplines, the problem with stock picking is that causation is more difficult to establish. The outcome follows the action instantaneously, whether you're shooting a basketball or writing a computer program. A ball either enters the hoop or does not. Programs either function properly or they don't.

In contrast, when picking stocks, you must wait for the outcome of your decision. It can take years for the feedback cycle.

And the return you finally receive must be contrasted with the return of investing in an index fund, such as the S&P 500. In other words, you could still lose money in relative terms even if you win money in absolute terms.

What's more, the outcome of your choice could not even be related to the reasons you first considered it. Take GameStop as an example. As the company's operations improved, you acquired the stock in late 2020 with the expectation that the price would rise.

Consider how frequently stock pickers experience this since there is a far less clear connection between their choices and the outcomes. Was the increase in the stock a result of a change you had anticipated or was it a result of a different change? How about when the mood of the market turns against you? Invest farther and make more purchases, or think again.

As a stock picker, these are just a handful of the queries you must ask yourself before making any investing choices. Existential dread may pervade in an unending manner. Despite your best efforts, do you understand what is happening?

The response is an unambiguous "yes" for some people. For argument's sake, let's assume that the top 10% of stock pickers and the worst 10% of stock pickers can easily determine their skill level (or lack thereof). This suggests a 20% probability that we could determine a stock picker's skill level and an 80% chance that we couldn't if we chose one randomly! This suggests that it would be challenging for 4 out of 5 stock pickers to demonstrate their skill.

The existential crisis I'm referring to is this one. Why would you want to engage in a game (or pursue a career) in which you cannot demonstrate your abilities? It's okay if you're doing it for fun. Take a little of your money, and start playing. But why devote so much time to something where your talent is difficult to assess if you aren't doing it for fun?

And even if you are among the best 10% of investors who can prove their stock-choosing prowess, your problems continue. For instance, what transpires if you unavoidably go through a period of poor performance? After all, poor performance won't happen if it doesn't happen.

Just imagine how tense this must be when it eventually occurs. Yes, you were skilled in the past, but how about now? Is your underperformance a typical slump that even the best investors go through, or have you lost your edge? It's never easy to lose touch with anything, but it's especially difficult when you're unsure whether you've done so.

Stock pickers may be ignoring these hazards unknowingly.

Also, I don't have anything against stock pickers; nevertheless, I do. This distinction is quite important. By maintaining reasonable efficiency in prices, knowledgeable stock pickers offer a useful service to markets. Stock picking, however, is an approach to investing that has burned far too many novice investors. My friends have experienced it. My family has witnessed it. Hopefully, it won't occur to you as well.

I'm aware that I won't be able to persuade every stock picker to alter their behavior, which is a good thing. People must continue to evaluate businesses and allocate their capital appropriately. If you are debating it, take this as a wake-up call. Playing a game that requires so much chance shouldn't be continued. Life already has enough luck enough

Chapter 11

Is Buying the Dip a Reliable Investment Strategy?

A legitimate strategy for trying to "play" the stock market is to buy the drop. But there's more to this investing approach than meets the eye.

Although buying the dip is a sound investment strategy, it can take time, and there are no assurances that you'll ultimately be profitable.

Share values typically decrease when the American stock market is down (as it has been during 2022). Purchasing stocks at a discount, or "buying the dip," may be a wise financial move if the stock's share price climbs to a level higher than what you paid for it initially.

While some investors may find success with this, you should be aware of the signs to watch for before purchasing the dip. Additionally, you should assess whether or if this investing approach is more advantageous for you than other, more straightforward ones.

What is a dip, and why would I buy one?

Purchasing stock after a large price decline is known as buying the dip. The multibillionaire investor Warren

Buffett has increased his riches using this method of investing.

For instance, on January 3, 2022, Microsoft shares were selling for just over $334 a share, but by June 13, 2022, that share price had fallen to roughly $242. Therefore, if you had purchased Microsoft stock in June, you would have been buying the dip because you believed the price decline would be brief and the stock would eventually rise in value again.

Why would you want to buy stocks when they are down? Similar to why you would purchase a product that is on sale: it is cheaper, allowing you to get more for your money. Undoubtedly, everyone enjoys a good deal. For instance, if you had $5,000 to invest in Microsoft, you would be able to purchase 20 shares at the June 2022 price drop, as opposed to just approximately 15 at the January 2022 price.

Identify equities that are expected to rebound and climb in price when you buy the dip to maximize your chances of making a profit. Consider buying 20 Microsoft shares at a discount price of $242, or about $4,840. You would receive a return on your investment of nearly $1,840 if the stock rose to $334 per share.

How Do You Buy the Dip?

Profiting from the dip requires planning, even though it may seem simple. You need to time the market to identify when buying and selling a stock is best.

You can do several things to improve your chances of succeeding in market timing, but it still requires some degree of luck.

Observe market trends

The quarterly earnings report of a firm, national politics, Federal Reserve interest rates, and the general state of the economy are just a few of the variables that affect stock price variations. Examine the stock's performance and market trends before investing in a stock and buying the dip. The stock's moving average is what? What performance has the stock shown over the past hour, week, or month?

It would be best if you didn't necessarily acquire shares when they first begin a negative trend because even though the share price may have already reached an all-time low, it could still decline further. It can be a good idea to buy the dip when the share price trends upward.

Utilize a predictor or an indicator.

There are various signs to pay attention to that could help you choose which stocks to buy and when to buy the drop. Volume, momentum, and price movements for a stock are some examples of these indicators. Additionally, you can utilize predictive modeling to make future stock performance predictions based on past performance data. When buying the drop, stocks with the potential for higher long-term returns are preferable to those with lower short-term returns.

Put Limit Orders in Place to Secure Your Price

You can specify the price you're willing to pay for a stock when you place a limit order to purchase or sell it. Only when a stock's market price reaches the price you've specified will the limit order be carried out. For instance, if a stock is trading at $5 per share and you place a limit order for $3.50, your order will be carried out automatically if the share price falls to $3.50.

Consider using dollar-cost averaging.

A technique you might employ when purchasing the drop is dollar-cost averaging. Instead of purchasing an entire stock at once, it entails purchasing a portion several times when its price fluctuates. As an illustration, your profit would be $1,500 if you spent $3,000 on 150 shares at $20 each, and the stock price increased to $30.

With dollar-cost averaging, also known as averaging down, you would purchase 50 shares at $20 per share, another 17 shares when the price lowers to $15 per share, and another 24 shares when the price reduces to $11 per share. Therefore, if the stock's share price rose to $30, your profit would be more in the neighborhood of $6,240.

Is investing in the dip a wise move?

Buying the dip can be a profitable investment strategy if you play your cards well. Day traders could buy the dip before "selling the rip" when the stock price rises again. Long-term ownership of the stock, though, can be more profitable.

In the earlier example, the stock of Microsoft had an annualized return of 25.51%, exceeding the historical average annual rate of return for the stock market of 10%. Once its stock price rises, Microsoft shares may have a better chance of turning a profit.

Advantages of buying the dip

The dip purchase might have some benefits if you play the game properly.

Get Better Returns

You will likely make a good profit if the price goes up, and you can sell your shares at a higher price because you are buying stock during a dip period when you can receive a lower price.

Lessen the cost basis.

Cost basis, the initial value of a stock, is used to compute capital gains taxes. When you purchase a stock at a discount, your cost basis is lower, allowing you to purchase more shares for the same investment and increase your margin of possible profit.

When selling your shares, remember that the cost basis will impact the capital gains taxes you'll owe. You'll have to pay more taxes if your cost basis is lower and your sale price is higher. Your stock holding period has an impact on your capital gains taxes as well. You'll pay a greater capital gains tax rate if you own a stock for less than a year.

Surpass market performance

The S&P 500 Index is regarded as a performance standard against which the rest of the stock market is assessed. Its historical average return has been around 10%. Investors that surpass this mark are said to have "beaten the market." You can outperform the market if you're successful in generating large profits from buying the dip.

Cons of Purchasing the Dip

Investors should be aware of the drawbacks of this technique because buying the dip is only for some.
It isn't easy to time the market.
Market timing is challenging due to stock market volatility. It may not be profitable for you to buy the dip. The ups and downs of an unpredictable stock market are difficult to predict, even for the most seasoned investors.

Possible Slow Recovery

Never consider buying the dip to be a quick-money plan. Only when stock prices rise above or above their former levels, which could take some time, do you make money (if it happens).

Time Out of the Market Could Be Expensive

A well-known investing maxim is "time in the market is better than timing the market." If you want to profit from your investments, market experience is crucial. In a volatile stock market, holding onto your assets could still result in a higher long-term return than trying to time the market and purchase the dip.

You might lose hundreds of dollars daily if your money isn't invested. According to a 2021 Fidelity analysis, $10,000 invested in the S&P 500 between January 1, 1980, and March 31, 2021, increased to $1.09 million. That nest egg would, however, decrease by 38% if just five of the greatest trading days were missed.

Alternative Investing Techniques

Although buying the dip might be beneficial, it is hazardous and necessitates a deeper understanding of basic investing principles to execute. Here are a few portfolio protection techniques you can consider as an alternative to buying the dip

Diversify Your Investment Portfolio

An excellent strategy to lower risk while investing through allocation is to diversify your portfolio with various investments. The performance of your portfolio as a whole will perform better with diversification than if you put all your eggs in one basket.

Chapter 12

How Soon Should You Sell?

Theoretically, the capacity to profit from stocks depends on two critical choices: buying at the right time and selling at the appropriate time. It would be best if you correctly carried out both of these choices to turn a profit. The decision to sell a stock is typically more challenging than buying it. You run the risk of forfeiting gains if you sell the stock too soon and it rises. You may miss your chance if you sell too soon and the stock falls. What can an investor do?

Many investors struggle to sell an asset, and occasionally this problem can be traced back to human nature's intrinsic propensity for greed. However, there are techniques you can employ to determine when it is (and isn't) a suitable moment to sell.

Selling Stocks Is Tough

Here is a far too typical scenario: Shares of stock are purchased at $25 to be sold at $30. You choose to wait for a few more dollars of gains once the stock reaches $30. As soon as the stock passes $32, greed precedes logic. The stock price abruptly decreases to $29 again. Just wait until it reaches $30 once more, you tell yourself. This never occurs. Once it reaches $23, you give up out of irritation and sell it at a loss.

In this situation, emotion and greed have triumphed over reason. Although you only lost $2 per share, when the price reached its high, you might have made a profit of $7.

The essential question is why the investor is selling or not selling, and it may be better to disregard these paper losses than to agonize over them. Consider using a limit order, which will automatically sell the stock when it hits your target price, to eliminate human nature from the equation. You won't even have to observe the price of that stock fluctuate. When your sell order is placed, you'll receive a notification.

There are a few intrinsic reasons to sell a stock, i.e., reasons related to the stock or markets. In addition, the investor might be motivated to sell for unrelated reasons concerning their finances or way of life. Occasionally, a mix of intrinsic and external variables may lead to the sell choice.

Let's first take a look at some internal motivations or influences.

Intrinsic Motives to Sell

• When the first purchase was a mistake: Most seasoned investors have probably encountered this circumstance at some point. You've been witnessing this stock, or more likely a meme stock, making incredible increases every day, so you finally decide to suspend your skepticism and foolishly place a huge purchase order for the stock. But as soon as you do, you understand that you most likely erred. Selling the stock would be the wisest move in this scenario, even if it meant a slight trading loss. And to prevent making the same error again, fight the urge to go after hot stocks that are barely making it, as doing so could cost you money.

• When the price increases noticeably: It's not always a good idea to sell a stock just because its value has increased. In some situations, the company's fundamentals may support the price increases (for instance, if investors increase sales and earnings more quickly than anticipated). In other instances, however, the price can have experienced exponential increases only as a result of speculation or for other causes, such as takeover rumors or a short squeeze. In these situations, the investor would do well to conduct some research to try and determine the cause of the stock gains and, depending on the results, either sell the entire position or sell part of the position and place a stop order to sell the remaining portion if it trades below a certain price. The decision to sell a stock becomes more important as its recent gains contribute to your entire portfolio. If you purchased 1,000 shares of a biotech stock at $5 per share, for instance, when the value of your entire portfolio was $25,000, that stock would have made up 20% of your portfolio. If, after three months, the biotech stock quadrupled on encouraging trial findings while the rest of your portfolio remained the same, it would now make up 50% of your portfolio. Given the potential harm to your portfolio, if the stock reversed most of its advance, it could be wise to sell some of your shares and take a portion of the winnings in this circumstance.

• If a stock hits your price objective: Have you ever owned a stock that had been in a slump for years but had recently found new life and was trading at your entry price? It would be best if you hadn't been holding on to that loser for so long in the first place, but that's a topic for another time. If you committed to yourself that you would sell the stock if it ever returned to your purchase price, get rid of it immediately. Similarly, why not sell all of a stock if it reaches a level it traded too briefly in the past? You always planned to sell if it did so again, or would you consider doing so to avoid missing out on another opportunity? Because of the following

• When a stock trades near a technical turning point: When a stock trades close to, then breaks below, a multiyear low, it frequently portends further losses in the future. Selling the stock in this scenario can be a good idea as soon as the technical level is broken on the downside. Similarly, suppose a stock breaks through a significant resistance level to the upside. In that case, it may indicate further gains and a wider trading range, which suggests it could be better to sell some of the position rather than the entire investment. Technical analysts often watch stock price charts to spot other signals, such as moving stock crosses.

• When a stock's fundamentals worsen: A stock's fundamentals might suffer for various reasons, including slower sales or profits growth, heightened competition, rising expenses, declining margins, or just value. A company's quarterly earnings report or occasionally "guidance" given before an earnings report may provide the first indication of deteriorating fundamentals.

The market typically reacts swiftly and unequivocally to bad news from a company, such as missed profit targets or dropped future guidance, with the stock likely to fall by double digits. In these circumstances, the investor must decide if the deterioration in the stock's fundamentals is short-term or long-term. Since this is not a simple operation, it could be better to sell the position and leave it initially, then determine if it should be taken back later.

• When a competing company releases negative news: Frequently when a bellwether company in a given industry publishes earnings below expectations, the troubles afflicting that sector may be brought to light. Unless you are certain that the sector's problems won't impact your stock, you should consider selling any shares in a firm in that industry.

• When the market appears shaky: Although this is not an easy process and is certainly not a recommendation to engage in market timing, there are occasions when the general market appears overextended, and it makes sense to trim the weaker companies in your portfolio at such times. Stocks of corporations with a high debt load or a precarious financial condition may experience a rapid decline in value.

Extrinsic Motives for Selling

• Financial factors: These can cover a wide range of factors relating to the investor's finances. For instance, a stock may have increased so substantially relative to the other investments in the portfolio (as in the case of the biotech stock discussed above) that the investor may need to rebalance it to restore equilibrium. Or the investor might want to sell a stock to record a loss for taxation. The desire for cash to invest in a rival investment, like real estate, maybe another justification for selling a stock. Such monetary justifications are fairly persuasive when used to sell a stock.

• Lifestyle changes: These factors are also valid justifications for selling stock. Younger investors may think about liquidating all or a portion of their holdings to put a down payment on a home or car. To wind down the equity portion of their portfolios and lower their risk exposure, investors close to retirement may sell equities. Additionally, parents are permitted to sell assets in tax-advantaged plans designated for particular goals, including their kids' education.

Chapter 13

How do the majority of investors respond to a crisis?

Regardless of the crisis type, there is always a lot of talk about the most recent developments, and this talk has an impact on investors. Investors frequently panic during times of crisis and begin selling their equity holdings, even if they end up losing money. Even though selling in a panic is frequently a bad choice, it frequently occurs due to the intense dread of suffering more losses.

Finding acceptable investments during these times might be challenging, even though you might not make a panic sale. When investing during a crisis, you should be aware of issues, including excessive equity market volatility and the possibility of a double-dip recession.

Presently, the crisis unfolding in Ukraine is following a similar trend. The general market has recovered greatly since the initial drop in Indian stock markets. Still, there is undoubtedly a great deal of uncertainty surrounding the prospects of investments made during the current crisis. Let's take a closer look at the effect of war on equity investments to get a clearer picture of how the current crisis might develop.

How does war affect equity markets?

War has a detrimental effect on the majority of asset classes, sectors, and industries. This is because war causes trade snarls, sanctions, higher prices, tariffs, and a shortage of raw resources. These elements, taken together, may cause many companies' equity share prices to decline by 10–30%.

For instance, amid the ongoing conflict between Ukraine and Russia, the cost of necessities, including wheat, cooking oil, nickel, natural gas, and petroleum, has significantly skyrocketed. This is because Russia and Ukraine export these goods to other countries, and the ongoing conflict has seriously disrupted supply.

The world's economies, including India's, will be impacted in the short-, medium-, and long-term due to this unexpected rise in commodity prices worldwide. There is another explanation for the correction in equity prices during times of crisis, aside from the shortage of commodities and rising input costs. This is connected to investors' perceptions and concerns over future equity market corrections.

How Should I Choose Investments During a Crisis?

Any economic, geopolitical, or socioeconomic crisis presents some chances to increase your fortune. In reality, historical data demonstrates that, as long as investors make prudent investment decisions, times of crises frequently aid investors in generating excess returns. Of course, the main cause of this is how investors react to crises.

Investors frequently shift their holdings to markets, businesses, and asset classes that are viewed as "safe" when a crisis emerges. These include gold, consumer goods, utilities, and technology. There is no assurance that these investments will contribute to the long-term creation of wealth, even though they can assist reduce equity portfolio losses to some extent.

Some more knowledgeable investors might choose a different route and short equities or index futures. A short seller can profit from indexes declining or share prices dropping. In plain English, short sellers borrow shares they do not already own and then sell them in the hopes that they would eventually be offered for sale at a lower price. This method of profiting from declining markets is only suitable for some investors because short-selling transactions are more complicated than purchasing and redeeming Mutual Fund units.

How Should I Invest When the Market Is Down?

You can purchase high-quality stocks at low prices while the equity markets are experiencing a decline. In a time of crisis, you must take into account the following important factors to choose the best high-quality stocks:

1. Invest in businesses that offer necessary products and services.

Choosing stocks of businesses that offer critical goods and services during times of crisis is often a wise choice. This is because industries that deal with necessities and everyday goods, like soap, milk, pharmaceuticals, rice, etc., perform better during crises. People can delay purchases of other goods or services, but that is not an option regarding necessities or items for daily use.

The same goes for businesses that cater to discretionary consumer markets like jewelry, cars, hospitality and entertainment, travel, etc. These companies' stock may trade at a significant discount during a crisis, but such companies often take longer to recover and thrive after a crisis.

2. Look for businesses that manage their supply chains.
During times of war, supply chain disruptions are to be
expected. Therefore, it is only natural for many businesses
to experience production-impacting shortages of raw
materials. Companies that manage their supply chain have
a substantial advantage in such situations.
Businesses using direct distributors can frequently
normalize their supply chain more quickly than
businesses using wholesalers. Similarly, businesses that
run their B2C channels—such as showrooms, diagnostic
centers, etc.—are better equipped to recover quickly than
those that rely on a third party.

3. Pick businesses that value their stakeholders
How a firm manages its stakeholders' interests is another
aspect to consider when investing in a crisis. It is a sign of
a good financial position if a business can offer extra
credit or working capital loans to its vendors, vendors,
and distributors during a crisis.
Compared to its financially weaker competitors, a
company with a robust balance sheet is better positioned
to weather a crisis. Additionally, the number of market
participants declines throughout the crisis. In that case,

businesses with a strong balance sheet may record large increases in market share by the time the crisis is finished.

4. Businesses Set Up to Gain Market Share

Whenever there is a crisis, unorganized players typically lose market share to organized ones. By contrast, weak companies deteriorate and may even go out of business, whereas strong organizations grow stronger due to a crisis.

To fill the supply chain gap, you need to invest in a business that operates in a highly demanded industry. By upping its advertising budget during tough times, such a business can get a bigger market share and establish itself as a premium brand.

Conclusion

In conclusion, investing is essential to personal finance because it allows individuals to grow their wealth and achieve their financial goals. From saving for retirement to funding education and buying a home, investing can be a powerful tool to help people achieve their financial objectives.

Investing involves allocating resources to a project to generate income or profit. What you hope to achieve and your sensitivity to risk influence the investment you select. Low risk typically results in lesser returns, and high risk typically results in higher returns. Stocks, bonds, property, precious metals, and other assets are all eligible for investment. Money, assets, digital currencies, or other forms of exchange can all be used for investing. Stocks, bonds, mutual funds, and real estate are examples of the various investment vehicles available. Each one has a unique set of risks and potential benefits.

Investing is an ongoing journey that requires ongoing learning and adaptation. Staying informed about market trends, economic indicators, and new investment opportunities is crucial to making informed decisions and optimizing investment returns. With the right knowledge and approach, investors can make informed decisions that align with their goals and achieve long-term financial security.

One way to stay informed is to follow financial news and market analysis. Many financial news outlets, both traditional and digital, provide up-to-date information on market trends, economic indicators, and new investment opportunities. Following financial experts on social media and subscribing to newsletters can provide valuable insights and analysis.

Another important aspect of successful investing is developing a sound investment strategy. This involves setting clear financial goals, assessing risk tolerance, and determining an appropriate asset allocation. A diverse portfolio that includes a mix of asset classes and investment options can help manage risk and optimize returns over the long term.

Risk management is also critical to successful investing. This includes diversifying investments across different asset classes, managing portfolio volatility, and keeping a long-term perspective to avoid making rash decisions in response to short-term market fluctuations. Setting stop-loss orders, regularly rebalancing portfolios and avoiding investments too good to be true are all ways to manage risk and optimize investment returns.

Investing can also have tax implications, with different types of investments subject to different tax rules. For example, capital gains on stocks and mutual funds held for over a year are typically taxed at a lower rate than short-term capital gains or ordinary income. Understanding these tax rules can help investors optimize their investment returns while minimizing their tax liabilities.

It's also important to note that investing is not a one-size-fits-all approach. Each individual's financial situation and goals are unique, and no single investment strategy or approach is right for everyone. Consulting with a financial advisor can help investors develop a personalized investment plan that aligns with their goals and risk.

Market volatility is another important factor to consider when investing. Stock prices can fluctuate significantly over short periods, and individual companies can experience significant changes in value due to news events or market sentiment. Managing risk by diversifying investments across different sectors and asset classes, setting stop-loss orders, and regularly rebalancing portfolios can help investors minimize the impact of market volatility on their overall investment returns.

Interest rates are also an important factor to consider when investing. Changes in interest rates can impact different investments in different ways. For example, rising interest rates can make bonds less attractive while making cash or short-term investments more attractive. Conversely, falling interest rates can make bonds more attractive while making stocks or real estate more attractive.

Finally, it's important to note that investing involves costs and fees that can impact investment returns. These costs can include brokerage fees, commissions, and fund management fees. Understanding these costs and fees, and seeking out low-cost investment options, can help investors maximize their investment returns over the long term.

Successful investing involves staying informed about economic and political events, managing risk, and optimizing investment returns based on current market conditions. By taking a long-term perspective, diversifying investments across different sectors and asset classes, and minimizing costs and fees, investors can achieve their financial goals and build long-term wealth.